THIS BOOK BELONGS TO:

This book is dedicated to my children –
Vince and Sagebelle.

MONEYTOPIA
SAVING

Written by
Dr. Shanshan Peer

Illustrated by
Jelena Stupar

Welcome to Moneytopia,
where money is called *topians*.

Here, everyone learns all about money from a very young age. That's because understanding how money works is so important!

This week at school, Ms. Kitty is teaching her class about *saving* money.

Ms. Kitty smiled. "Your parents are responsible for getting you the things you need: food, clothing, a place to live. Needs are things we *must* have. But sometimes we want things that we don't need. Wants are things that we'd *like* to have, but that we could do without."

NEEDS: ESSENTIALS, MUST-HAVES

WANTS: NICE-TO-HAVES

SAVINGS = EARNING - WANTS - NEEDS

"I've got it," Chuck shouted. "What if we save up our money for a space-themed class party? And Ms. Kitty can teach us all about space."

"And it's a good, achievable saving goal. The key to savings is to have a good plan and to create a budget. Setting a budget means deciding how much of what you earn can be spent, and how much needs to be saved. If you stick to your budget, you can achieve your saving goal."

$$50 \div 10 = 5$$

EARNING = 10 TOPIANS/WEEK

SAVING GOAL = 5 TOPIANS/WEEK

BUDGET = 10 − 5 = 5 TOPIANS/WEEK

That *is* a good idea, Chuck

"Now let's see. You have 10 weeks until the end of this term. If each of you saves 50 topians by then, we can have an outer space class party."

The first week, Lexie earned 10 topians for selling lemonade. She was so excited, she raced to the candy store to celebrate.

"Six topians?" Chuck asked. "But you only earned 10. What happened to saving for the class party?"

Lexie blushed. "I guess I forgot," she admitted. "It's okay. I'll save extra next week."

But the week after, Lexie bought balloons, and the week after that she bought a bouncy ball.

By the end of the third week, Zoey and Chuck had each saved 15 topians.

Lexi had only saved 8 topians.

"What would make you happier?" Zoey asked. "A class party or candy, balloons, and bouncy balls?"

"Learning about outer space is my dream!" Lexie answered.

I want a space party more than anything!

"Don't worry. We'll help you!" Chuck reassured Lexie. "There are still 7 weeks left. If you can save 6 topians per week, you will be able to catch up."

Lexie wrote down her spending versus her budget. "I guess I *have* been spending too much," she said. "But I can do better. Let's see. If I earn 10 topians per week, and I need to save 6 topians per week, that leaves me with . . . four topians to spend each week. Hmmm. That's not so bad!"

Over the next three weeks, Lexie did much better. Each week she earned 10 topians selling lemonade. And each week she rewarded herself with candies, balloons, or toys.

But this time, Lexie was careful about her spending. She limited herself to four topians, and not a topian more.

Once or twice Lexie almost bought something more expensive, but she stopped herself. Even though it upset her not to get everything she wanted, she knew that the class party would be worth it.

Then, a few weeks before the party, Lexie, Chuck, and Zoey were walking home when they passed an ice cream stand. Chuck and Zoey hadn't spent any money that week, and each got themselves an ice cream.

Lexie hated feeling left out. Why should they have ice cream when she didn't? So she decided to buy herself an ice cream, too.

Lexie's mom sat down beside her. "Sometimes saving is about prioritization," she said.

Lexie decided that was good advice. Instead of carrying the money she earned around with her, she put the six topians she needed to save into her savings account as soon as she got paid. Then, she used the leftover to buy the things that she wanted.

The plan worked! Lexie never broke her budget again. And she was able to save 50 topians in time!

At the party, Ms. Kitty's students learned so much about the space. They studied rocket ships, planets, satellites, and moons.

The party was everything they could have dreamed about . . . and so much more!

Download free printables at
www.drmamapeer.com/books

@DrMamaPeer   Kind Grit Books   KindGrit
@KindGritBooks
#Moneytopia

Made in the USA
Las Vegas, NV
11 June 2022

50091499R10021